101 HILARIOUS CLEAN JOKES & RIDDLES FOR KIDS

Laugh Out Loud With These Funny and Clean Riddles & Jokes For Children (WITH 30+ PICTURES)!

Johnny Riddle

Table of Contents

INTRODUCTION

First joke: *Why didn't the leopard want to play hide and seek anymore?*

Answer: He was always spotted!

Or how about this one:

Two girls were having a coffee at Starbucks, when one said to the other: I've named my toilet "the Jim" instead of "the John." That way, it sounds so much better when I say I go to "the Jim" in the morning!

Thank you for picking up a copy of '*101 Hilarious Clean Jokes & Riddles For Kids*'.

Are you ready to crack up about these funny jokes?

Laughter is good for you!

You probably already knew that. I mean, who doesn't feel good when they laugh, right?

But did you know that laughter is associated with all these health benefits?

Laughter:

- relaxes your body
- boosts your immune system
- triggers the release of feel-good hormones, such as endorphins
- protects your heart

When you're reading these jokes with your kids, you're *also* working on their health!

Sounds good, right?

If you're looking for a good laugh, you've come to the right place!

This book is jam-packed with:

- 100+ hilarious clean jokes, and
- 30+ funny illustrations

that all kids will love.

So, I hope you and your kids are ready to *roar with laughter*: **let's get started with the first joke!**

101 HILARIOUS CLEAN JOKES & RIDDLES FOR KIDS

1.

A teacher asks her class: "Let's say I gave you two dogs, two more dogs, and then another two dogs; how many would you have?"

Wilma answers: "Seven."

Teacher: "No, Wilma, let me repeat the question... If I gave you 2 dogs, 2 more dogs and then another 2, how many would you have in total?"

Wilma: "7."

Teacher, getting frustrated now: "Pff, OK...Let's try this another way. If I gave you two bananas, two more bananas, and then another two, how many bananas would you have?"

Wilma: "Six."

Teacher: "Exactly! Now, if I gave you two dogs, two more, and another two; how many would you have?"

Wilma: "Seven!"

Teacher: "Wilma, where on earth do you get seven from?!"

Wilma: "Because I already have a dog at home!"

2.

Q: Why wasn't the blonde able to add 5 + 10 on her calculator?

A: Because she couldn't figure out where the "10" button was!

3.

Q: What do you call a pig that practices karate?

A: A pork chop.

4.

A traveler sits down in a restaurant to get lunch. All of a sudden, a giraffe walks in, buys a strawberry ice cream and leaves.

The traveler is astounded: "Wow, that's so strange!"

The restaurant manager: "Yeah, I agree, up until today he always ordered chocolate ice cream."

5.

While mending fences out on the range, a very religious cowboy lost his favorite Bible. He was devastated…

However, three weeks later, a horse walked up to him, carrying his Bible in its mouth!

The cowboy was astonished; he couldn't believe it! He took the precious book out of the horse's mouth, thanked him profusely, went on his knees and exclaimed: "It's a miracle!"

To which the horse replied: "Not really. Your name is written inside the cover."

6.

Q: What do you call an alligator wearing a blue vest?

A: An investigator!

7.

Joshua: "Did you the news item about the kidnapping at school?"

Shane: "Yes, I saw it. You don't need to worry about it though. He just woke up."

8.

Mr. and Mrs. Huddlefield had a happy marriage, with two sons. Don't ask why, but when they were born they gave them very unique names: they named their first son 'Trouble', and the other son 'Mind Your Own Business'.

The boys were best friends. One day, they decided to play 'Hide and Seek'. 'Trouble' hid while 'Mind Your Own Business' counted to sixty. After he finished counting, 'Mind Your Own Business' began looking for his brother. He started with bushes, small corners, and even garbage cans. When he couldn't find him, he started looking in and under cars.

This was when he caught the attention of a police officer on duty.

The officer approached him, and asked: "Hey there, what are you doing?" "Playing a game," the boy replied.

"What is your name?" the officer then asked. "Mind Your Own Business." Furious, and with a raised voice, the police offer then asked, "Are you looking for trouble?!"

To which the boy replied, "Yes, I am!"

9.

One day, a little girl is sitting at the kitchen table when she asks her father, "How were people born?"

Her father replied, "Well, Adam and Eve made babies, then their babies became adults and made babies, and that's how people were born."

That afternoon, the girl was having tea with her mother and asked her the same question. Her mom answered, "At first, we were monkeys, but then we evolved to become like we are now."

When her father got home from work, the little girl ran to him and yelled, "Dad, you lied to me!"

After she had explained what happened, her father replied, "I didn't lie to you. Your mom was only talking about her side of the family."

10.

Q: Can a kangaroo jump higher than the Statue of Liberty?

A: Of course! The Statue of Liberty can't jump, silly.

11.

Q: Why did the blonde woman run around her bed?

A: Because she was trying to catch up on her sleep!

12.

Q: A boy volcano was located next to a girl volcano.
What did he say to her?

A: "I lava you..."

13.

Q: Why is six so scared of seven?

A: Because seven "ate" nine.

14.

Q: Why are the hairs of bees so sticky?

A: Because they use honey combs for it!

15.

Q: What do you call a dog magician?

A: A labracadabrador!

16.

Knock, Knock!

Who is there?

Chicken.

Chicken who?

Chicken your pockets, maybe you'll find your keys *there*!

17.

An elementary school teacher wants to educate her class about animals.

Teacher: "Children, what does a pig give you?"

Joshua: "Bacon!"

Teacher: "Very good, Joshua! Class, what does a chicken give you?"

Linda: "Eggs!"

Teacher: "Well done, Linda! Anyone else: what does the cow give you?"

Larry: "Homework!"

Teacher: "..."

18.

Two moms talk about their sons, over a cup of coffee.

Mother 1: "I really have the perfect son, you know?"

Mother 2: "Is that so...Tell me, does he ever come home late?"

Mother 1: "No, never."

Mother 2: "Does he drink beer?"

Mother 1: "No, he never even had a glass of alcohol."

Mother 2: "Does he smoke?"

Mother 1: "No, he never lit a cigarette in his life!"

Mother 2: "Wow, I'm impressed! I guess you really do have the perfect son...How old is he?"

Mother 1: "He will be six months old next Friday."

19.

Q: What does a computer eat when it's hungry?

A: Microchips!

20.

Q: Why shouldn't you give a cat the remote control when you're watching Netflix?

A: Because he always hit the 'paws' button!

21.

Q: Why do giraffes make terrible dance partners?

A: They've got two left feet!

22.

Q: How did the eggs leave the highway?

A: They went through the eggs-it.

23.

Did you read the newspaper, about the woman whose whole left-side was cut off?

She's all right now...

24.

I have this friend, and he thinks he is really smart. One day, he tried to convince me that an onion is the only food that can make you cry.

So I grabbed a coconut and threw it at his face...

25.

A young boy came home from school, with a black eye. "What happened?", his mother asked

"I had a big fight with my classmate," the boy replied, "He called me a sissy."

"And, what did you do?", the mother asked.

The little boy said, "I hit him with my purse!"

26.

Here's a trick in case you ever get cold: go to the corner of a room and stand there for a while.

Normally, they are around 90 degrees...

27.

Q: What do you think difference is between an acoustic guitar and a fish?

A: You can tune a guitar, but you cannot tuna fish!

28.

Q: Why did all the students in class kids eat their homework?

A: Because their teacher told them: "It's a piece of cake!"

29.

Q: What do you get when you cross a Golden Retriever with a telephone?

A: A golden receiver.

30.

One day, a woman walked into a lawyer's office and said, "My colleague owes me $400 and she won't pay up. I'm here for legal advice; what should I do?"

The lawyer thought about it for a few seconds, and then asked: "Do you have any proof you loaned her the money?". "Unfortunately, I don't," the woman replied.

"OK, then here's what you should do. Write her an email asking her for the $4,000 she owes you," the lawyer said.

"Huh, she only owes me $400, though" the woman replied.

"Indeed. That's what she will reply. And that email will be your proof!"

31.

Q: If you have 15 oranges in one hand and 12 bananas in the other, what do you have?

A: Big hands!

32.

John: "Wow, I just fell off a 40 ft. ladder."

Hank: "Oh my, are you okay?"

John: "Yeah. It's a good thing I fell off the first step."

33.

A woman woke up in the morning, next to her husband. She rolled over and told him, "You know what I just dreamed? You would give me a pearl necklace! What do you think that means?"

"Tonight, you will know," he replied.

That evening, the man came home and gave his wife a small gift-wrapped package and gave it to his wife.

Delighted, his wife opened it to find a book entitled "Dreams: What Do They Mean?"

34.

A science teacher wants to test if his students remember what he told them yesterday

Teacher: "Class, can anyone tell me what the chemical formula for water is?"

George: "HIJKLMNO."

Teacher: "George, what on earth are you talking about?"

George: "Yesterday, you told us it is H to O!"

35.

Q: What happens to the car of a frog car when it breaks down?

A: The car gets toad away.

36.

Q: What did the big chimney say to the little chimney?

A: "Sorry kid, you're too young to smoke."

37.

Q: What is a cat's favorite breakfast?

A: Mice Krispies!

38.

Q: If you were to cross a dog and a calculator, what would you get?

A: A friend you can count on!

39.

Q: What would you get when you cross a shark and an elephant?

A: Swimming trunks!

40.

Three men are all in the hospital, in the waiting room, waiting for their wives to give birth to their babies.

After a few hours have passed, a nurse approaches one of the men and says, "Congratulations, sir! You are now the father of twins." "Wow, that's strange," answers the man. "I work for the Minnesota Twins. Guess I have a cool story to tell at work!"

An hour passes, and the nurse comes back to the second man. "Congratulations," she says, "You just became the father of quadruplets!" After he recovered from the shock, the man responds "That's so odd, I am the manager of a Four Seasons hotel!"

Seconds later, the last man starts to freak out, banging his head against the wall. "What's the matter?" the others ask.

The man replies, "I work in a 7-Up factory!"

41.

One day, a man was driving on a country road when he looked out of the window and noticed a pig running alongside his car. He was amazed to see the pig keeping up with him: he was driving 40 mph! So, he accelerated to 50. But the pig stayed right next to him. Even more astonished, he now sped up to 60 mph, but the pig not only kept up with him, it even passed him!

Then the man noticed something peculiar: the pig had 5 legs. He decided to follow the pig and finally ended up at a farm. When he got out of his car and looked around, he was even more shocked: all the pigs on this farm had 5 legs!

He approached the farmer and asked: "Why do all these pigs have 5 legs?"

The farmer replied: "Well, I figured: 5 legs is more pig meat. So, I decided to breed a five-legged pig. I'm going to be a rich!"

Then the man asked him how the pigs tasted. Then the farmer said, with a sad expression on his face: "I don't know, I haven't caught one yet..."

42.

Shaun walked into the doctor's office for a health checkup.

"I have some good news and some bad news," the doctor said.

"I'll start with the good news: you only have 24 hours left to live."

"That's the good news?!", Shaun replies, with panic in his eyes.

"Yes," the doctor responds, "The bad news is that I should have told you this yesterday."

43.

Teacher: "Is there anyone in this class who thinks he's stupid? If so, please stand up!"

Everybody remains seated.

Teacher: "Come one class, surely there are some stupid students here!"

Rachel stands up.

Teacher: "Oh, Rachel, do you think you're stupid?"

Rachel: "No, teacher. I just feel bad that you're the only one standing..."

44.

Q: Why is it a bad idea to write a letter with a broken pencil?

A: Because it is pointless!

45.

Q: Why is Peter Pan always flying through the sky?

A: Because he Neverlands!

46.

Q: What type of nails do carpenters not like to hit?

A: Fingernails!

47.

In the car on the way back from baseball practice, a little boy asks his father, "Dad, how do parents pick the names for their children?"

"Well, my boy," his father responds, "The night before the mother is scheduled to give birth, the father goes into the forest with his tent and a few beers, to camp for the night. It is tradition that, when he wakes up the next morning, the first thing he sees when he leaves his tent is what he will name his child. That's why I named your brother Flying Eagle.

What made you ask this question, Reindeer Poop?"

48.

Q: What do you call the security men keeping guard outside a Samsung shop?

A: Guardians of the Galaxy!

49.

Did you hear about the new restaurant that opened up downtown, called Karma?

There don't have a menu. You simply get what you deserve!

50.

Q: Why is it a good idea to go to a football game on a hot day?

A: Because there are a lot of fans!

51.

Q: What did the banana say, when he walked into the doctor's office?

A: "Doctor, I am not peeling well."

52.

Q: What did the left eye say to the right eye?

A: Between you and me, there is something that smells.

53.

One day, a man visited his friend. When he walked into the living room, he found his friend playing chess with a tiger.

Astonished, he watched the game for a couple of minutes. "I can't believe my eyes!" he exclaimed. "That is the smartest tiger I have ever seen."

To which his friend replied: "Mwoah, he's not that smart. I've beaten him three games out of five."

54.

Jerry: "Why do hippos wear pink nail polish?"

Monica: "I don't have a clue."

Jerry: "To hide in cherry trees."

Monica: "Come on, Jerry. I have never seen a hippo in a cherry tree."

Jerry: "See, it works!"

55.

Q: What do chickens serve to their friends at birthday parties?

A: Coop-cakes!

56.

Q: If a plane crashed on the border of the U.S. and Mexico, in which country would the survivors be buried?

A: In none of the two: you don't bury survivors!

57.

Q: Why is a vampire so easy to fool?

A: Because he is a sucker!

58.

One day, a woman walks into a store to get some groceries. When she's done, she goes to the clerk to pay. The clerk looks at her items and sees 3 tomatoes, yoghurt, a chocolate bar and cheese.

"Let me guess, you must be single," the clerk says.

The woman, surprised, answers, "Well yes, how can you tell?"

The clerk replies, "Because you're ugly."

59.

Q: What would you call a belt with a watch attached to it?

A: A waist of time!

60.

One day, a penguin walks in a shop and asks the clerk if they sell hazelnuts. The clerk says, "No, we don't sell hazelnuts." The penguin goes home and returns the next day, "Hello, do you sell hazelnuts?". Again, the clerk says they don't.

The penguin leaves the shop, and returns the very next day. "There he is again," says the clerk to himself. And sure enough, the penguin asks the clerk if they sell hazelnuts. This time though, the clerk is so fed up with this stupid penguin that he says, "No, penguin, we don't sell hazelnuts! And if you come back one more time and ask me this question again, I will nail your beak to the floor!"

The penguin goes home again. The clerk can't believe his eyes when he sees the penguin walk through the door again, the next day. This time, the penguin asks, "Do you have any nails?" The clerk says, "No, we don't have any nails."

"Okay, good," the penguin says, "Do you sell hazelnuts?"

61.

A man takes his Bulldog to the vet, because he is cross-eyed.

The vet says: "Let's have a look" and picks up the Bulldog to examine his eyes. After looking at his eyes for a while, the vet says: "I'm going to have to put him down."

"Wait, what?" the man replies, "Just because he is cross-eyed?"

Vet: "No, because he is really heavy!"

62.

One Saturday morning, a wife said to her husband: "Our dog is so smart. He brings in the daily newspapers every single morning!"

Her husband responded: "Yes, he's a great dog, but lots of dogs can do that."

"Yes, but we've never subscribed to any," the wife replied.

63.

Q: Why is it a bad idea to tell a joke to an egg?

A: Because it might very well crack up!

64.

A policeman stops a man in a car with a crocodile in the front seat. "What are you doing with that crocodile?", he asked, "You should take it to the zoo!"

The next week, the police officer sees the same man with the crocodile again in the front seat. This time, both are wearing sunglasses.

The policeman pulls the car over. "I thought you were going to take it to the zoo!" The man replied, "I did. We had such a great time we are going to the beach this weekend!"

65.

Q: What is even more amazing than a talking bear?

A: A spelling bee!

66.

Q: Two toilet rolls are sitting in a bar. What did the first toilet roll say to the other?

A: "People keep on ripping me off!"

67.

Q: What is orange and really bad for your teeth?

A: A brick.

68.

Teacher: "Class, who can tell me where the Declaration of Independence was signed?"

Jimmy: "At the bottom of the page!"

69.

Q: What's a dog's favorite kind of pizza?

A: Pupperoni.

70.

A cow went to the post office to send a telegram. He took out a blank form and wrote: "Moo. Moo. Moo. Moo. Moo. Moo. Moo. Moo. Moo."

When he was done, he gave it to the clerk. The clerk looked at the paper and said to the cow: "There are only 9 words here. We have a special offer: You could send another 'Moo' for the same price."

To which the cow replied: "Sorry, but that wouldn't make any sense at all!"

71.

Nurse: "Doctor, the invisible man just arrived for his 4pm appointment with you."

Doctor: "Please tell him I'm sorry, I can't see him right now."

72.

Q: What's a shark's favorite lunch dish?

A: Peanut butter and jellyfish sandwich!

73.

Knock, Knock.

Who's there?

Lettuce.

Lettuce who?

Lettuce in. It's freezing outside!

74.

Q: How can you use water to create light?

A: By cleaning the windows!

75.

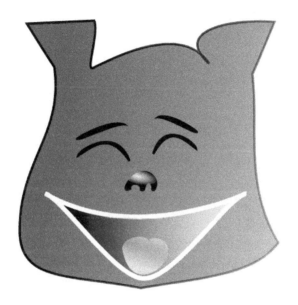

After not seeing one another for a couple of years, two old friends bump into each other at a basketball game.

Matthew: "What's up, bro, are you doing these days?"

Rob: "I'm a PHD."

Jerry: "Wow! That's crazy, you're a doctor, now?!"

Rob: "No, Pizza Home Delivery."

76.

One day, a man was walking in a shopping mall when he noticed a sign in a store window that said "Help Wanted."

The man didn't waste a second, ran in the store and yelled out, "What's wrong?"

77.

A zebra walks into a job center. "Wow, a talking zebra," says the clerk. "With your talent, I'm sure we can find you a gig in the circus."

"The circus?" says the zebra, disappointed: "What does a circus want with an accountant?"

78.

Q: What did one hat say to the other hat?

A: Stay here, I'll go on a head.

79.

Q: What type of book has no story, but lots of characters?

A: A telephone book!

80.

Q: Why does a seagull fly over the sea?

A: Because if he flew over the bay, he would be called a bagull!

81.

Q: What is a ninja's favorite kind of shoes?

A: Sneakers.

82.

A man took his guinea pig to the vet. The doctor shook his head as he looked at the guinea pig.

"I'm sorry, I'm afraid your guinea pig is dead" said the vet.

"Wait, what, how could you be so sure?" the man replied.

So, the vet left the room and come back with a Labrador Retriever. The dog stood up on its hind legs, sniffed the guinea pig and shook its head.

Next, the vet left the room again. This time, he came back with a cat. The cat also sniffed the guinea pig and also shook its head.

The vet said that the guinea pig was 100% dead. With the man still in shock, the vet handed him the bill. He looked at the bill, in disbelief: "$750, why $750?"

The vet replied "If you had believed me when I first said it, it would have been $100. But you didn't believe me. So, to confirm the death, you also had a lab report and a cat scan!"

83.

Q: What does a cat say when you step on its tail?

A: "Me-OW!"

84.

Mom walks in the living room, to find her son Adam crying.

She turns to her other son, angrily, and asks: "Zack, why did you kick your brother in the stomach?"

Zack: "It was pure accident, mom. He turned around..."

85.

A man runs into the office of a psychiatrist and says, "Doc, you have to help me! My wife thinks she's a chicken and I don't know what to do!"

The psychiatrist, still somewhat shocked from the man bursting into his office: "Yes, OK, I see. Tell me, how long has she had this condition?"

"One-and-a-half years," says the man.

"That long, you say?!", asked the psychiatrist, "Why didn't you come see me earlier?"

The man shrugs his shoulders and replies: "We needed the eggs."

86.

Q: Why didn't the sailors play cards on the boat?

A: Because the captain was on the deck.

87.

Q: Why does a pirate not know the alphabet?

A: He always get stuck at 'C'!

88.

Q: Why did the marathon runner stop listing to music during his runs?

A: Because he broke too many records!

89.

Q: What did one wall say to the other wall?

A: "I will see you at the corner!"

90.

Two buffalos are sitting on opposite sides of a river. One buffalo yells to the other: "How do I get to the other side of the river?"

To which the other buffalo replies: "You ARE on the other side!"

91.

Q: What is fuzzy, green, and if it fell out of a tree it would definitely kill you?

A: A pool table.

92.

Knock, Knock

Who's there?

Boo.

Boo who?

Please don't cry. It's only a joke.

93.

Q: What is a question that has a different answer each time you ask it?

A: 'What time is it?'

94.

Q: How did the frog die?

A: He Kermit suicide.

95.

Q: Of all the pets, which one makes the most noise?

A: A trumpet!

96.

A woman is on the train station, and approaches the station master.

Woman: "Excuse me, is this my train?"

Station Master: "No, Mam, it belongs to the railway company."

Woman, a bit taken aback: "That's funny, you got me there. However, what I mean to ask if I can take this train to Chicago."

Station Master: "No Mam, it's too heavy for that."

97.

A man in a movie theater noticed what looked like a goat sitting next to him. "Are you a goat?" asked the man, surprised. "Yes", said the goat.

"What are you doing at the movies?"

The goat replied, "Well, I liked the book."

98.

Knock, Knock.

Who's there?

Hatch.

Hatch who?

Bless you.

99.

Q: Why did the ants dance on top of the jam jar?

A: The lid read: 'Twist to open'!

100.

Q: How does one ocean say hello to another ocean?

A: He waves!

101.

A man is walking along a beach in California when he finds a bottle. He picks it up and rubs it. All of a sudden, a genie appears and says, "Hello stranger, this is your lucky day. I will grant you one wish!"

"Wow, this is my lucky day indeed," says the man, "My mom lives on Hawaii, and I never liked flying that much. Could you make a highway from Los Angeles all the way to Hawaii?" The genie replies, "Do you know how much of my power that would take?"

The man says, "Okay, okay, let me change my wish. I have had a lot of bad luck dating girls. Can you help me find a girl to date?"

The genie responds, "So, that highway: do you want that with two lanes or four lanes?"

BONUS JOKES

These are <u>11 bonus jokes</u> from my popular book *'101 Hilarious Animal Jokes'*.

Enjoy!

***

1.

A first-grade teacher was telling her students the story of the 2005 animated movie 'Chicken Little.' She got to the part when Chicken Little ran up to the farmer, saying: "The sky is falling. The sky is falling."

Then the teacher paused, looked around the class, and asked the kids what they thought the farmer said in reply.

One little boy raised his hand and said: "I think the farmer said: Holy cow, a talking chicken!"

Teacher: "Exactly! Now, if I gave you two dogs, two more, and another two; how many would you have?"

Wilma: "Seven!"

Teacher: "Wilma, where on earth do you get seven from?!"

Wilma: "Because I already have a dog at home!"

2.

The teacher asks the class to make a drawing of a cow in the grass.

After about 30 minutes, the teacher walks around to see the results. He pauses when he sees Johnny's drawing: "The assignment was to draw a cow and grass, Johnny, but I only see a cow on your drawing. Where is grass?"

Johnny: "The cow ate all the grass, teacher."

3.

Q: What did the waiter say to the dog when he brought out her food?

A: Bone appétit!

4.

Q: If a Transformer lived in the deep sea, what would you call it?

A: Octopus Prime!

5.

A King, who's is very fond of all kinds of animals and has its own zoo, hosts a Royal Dinner Party for all the important people in the country.

To impress his guests, he has asked his staff to put some of his most-loved animals in the party room.

One of the animals in the room, an Orangutan, lets out a loud fart.

The King turns to him and says: "How dare you fart in front of me!"

The Orangutan replies: "I'm terribly sorry, your Highness, I didn't realize it was your turn!"

6.

Knock, Knock.

Who's there?

Giraffe.

Giraffe who?

Giraffe something to eat? I'm super hungry!

7.

Did you hear about the owl who invented the Knock-Knock joke?

He won the no-bell prize!

8.

Q: What do you call a dog with a surround system?

A: A sub-woofer!

9.

Two friends were walking their dogs on a Friday afternoon. One had a Bulldog and the other had a Chihuahua.

Then the guy with the Bulldog said: "I'm thirsty, let's get a drink in that bar over there." To which his friend replied: "I don't think they will allow our dogs in there." The one with the Bulldog responded: "Just follow my lead, trust me."

The guy with the Bulldog put on a pair of sunglasses and walked into the bar.

The bouncer at the door said: "I'm sorry man, but there are no pets allowed inside." The man with the Bulldog replied: "But this is my guide dog, I am helpless without him!". Bouncer: "A Bulldog?"

The man replied: "Yeah, they're using Bulldogs now too, they're amazing!". Bouncer: "Okay, come on in."

The other man then also put on his sunglasses. He thought: a Chihuahua is even more unlikely to be a guide dog, but it's worth a try. So the bouncer stopped him, and said: "Sorry no pets allowed." To which the man replied: "This is my guide dog, I am lost without him." Bouncer: "Really, a Chihuahua?".

To which the man replied: "Whhaaat? They gave me a fricking Chihuahua?!"

10.

Q: What do you get when you cross a chicken with a Martian?

A: An eggs-traterrestrial!

11.

Q: Where do lizards go when their tails fall off?

A: The re-tail store!

***

This is the end of this bonus chapter.

Want to continue reading?

Then go to Amazon and search for "101 Animal Jokes."

Hope to see you there!

DID YOU LIKE THIS BOOK?

If you enjoyed this book, I would like to ask you for a favor. Please leave a review on Amazon!

Reviews are the lifeblood of independent authors. I know, you're short on time. But I would really appreciate even just a few sentences!

Your voice is important for this book to reach as many people as possible.

You can find the book by going to Amazon and:

- Checking your purchases, or
- Searching for "101 Hilarious Clean Jokes"

The more reviews this book gets, the more people will be able to find it and have a good laugh with these funny jokes!

***

IF YOU DID NOT LIKE THIS BOOK, THEN PLEASE TELL ME! You can email me at **feedback@semsoli.com**, to share with me what you did not like.

Perhaps I can change it.

A book does not have to be stagnant, in today's world. With feedback from readers like yourself, I can improve the book. So, you can impact the quality of this book, and I welcome your feedback. Help make this book better for everyone!

Thank you again for reading this book: I hope you had a good laugh!

JOKE BOOKS
BY
JOHNNY RIDDLE

101 HILARIOUS ANIMAL JOKES & RIDDLES FOR KIDS

WITH 35+ PICTURES!

Johnny Riddle

101 HILARIOUS
YO MAMA
JOKES

Laugh Out Loud With

These Funny Yo Momma

Jokes: So Bad, Even

Your Mum Will Crack Up!

JOHNNY RIDDLE

101 *HILARIOUS*
DUMB BLONDE
JOKES

WITH
35+
PICTURES!

Johnny Riddle